TWO FOOLISH CATS

Mr. Monkey

Tiger Cat Tabby Cat

Narrator

A PLAY BASED ON A TRADITIONAL STORY FROM JAPAN

Narrator: Once upon a time,
there were two cats
who lived in the hills in Japan.
One was a very large tiger cat,
and one was a small tabby cat.

They were good friends
until one day,
as they were walking over the hills,
they each found a newly baked rice cake.

3

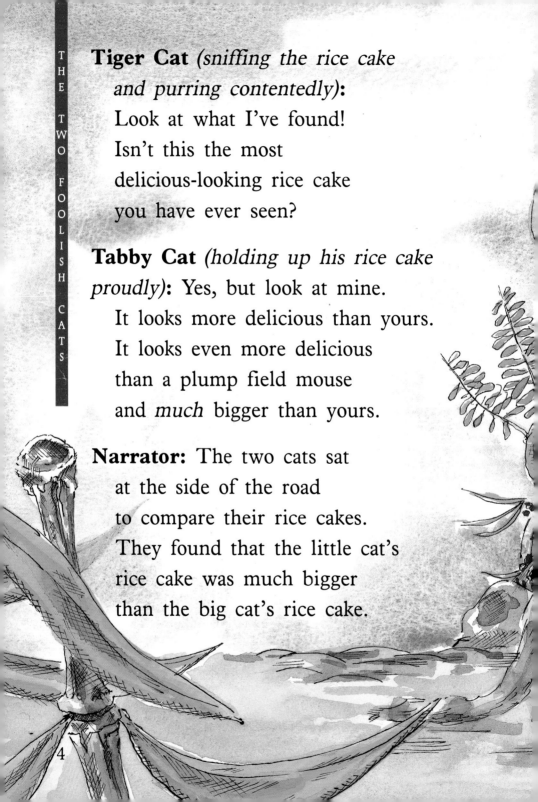

Tiger Cat (*sniffing the rice cake
and purring contentedly*)**:**
Look at what I've found!
Isn't this the most
delicious-looking rice cake
you have ever seen?

Tabby Cat (*holding up his rice cake
proudly*)**:** Yes, but look at mine.
It looks more delicious than yours.
It looks even more delicious
than a plump field mouse
and *much* bigger than yours.

Narrator: The two cats sat
at the side of the road
to compare their rice cakes.
They found that the little cat's
rice cake was much bigger
than the big cat's rice cake.

5

Tiger Cat *(full of importance)*:
That's not fair.
I'm much bigger than you are, so I should
have the bigger rice cake. Here, let's trade.

Tabby Cat *(growling and showing
his teeth)*: Oh no, no thank you.
Because I'm small,
I need more food than you do
so that I can grow as big as you.
I will *not* trade.

Tiger Cat *(beginning to lose his temper)*:
If you won't trade with me,
I'll fight you for it!

Tabby Cat: Just you try it!
I may be smaller than you
but I'm just as tough.
I found this rice cake and I'm keeping it!

Narrator: The two cats argued
and argued.
They hissed and yowled
for hours and hours.

Tiger Cat: This will never do.
We could go on arguing forever.
I know the wise monkey of the forest.
Let's go and see him
and ask him to decide
what is right and fair
for both of us.

Tabby Cat: Very well.
If we don't stop arguing soon,
our delicious rice cakes
will become hard and stale.

Narrator: The two cats went off
into the woods to search
for the monkey.

Tiger Cat and Tabby Cat
(*calling loudly together*
as they search through the woods):
Mr. Monkey, Mr. Monkey,
where are you?
We need you to help us decide
what is right and fair.
Mr. Monkey! Mr. Monkey!

Narrator: Suddenly, a voice above them
rings out loudly.

Mr. Monkey: I can hear you. I can hear you.
How can I help you?

Tiger Cat and Tabby Cat (*together*):
Oh, Mr. Monkey, wise Mr. Monkey,
we need you to help us decide
what is right and fair.

Mr. Monkey: I shall certainly do my best.
What's the problem?

Tabby Cat: We found these two rice cakes.
I found the bigger rice cake...

Tiger Cat: I found the smaller rice cake.
But because I'm bigger,
I should have the bigger rice cake.
Surely that is fair, Mr. Monkey.

Tabby Cat: No, that isn't fair.
I should have the bigger rice cake.
I'm small and I need more food.

Mr. Monkey: Aha! I see.
You were so right to ask me.
The answer is simple.
You must each have a rice cake
of exactly the same size.
I know I can help you.

Narrator: The cats nodded and smiled.
Mr. Monkey placed the rice cakes
on his scales.

Mr. Monkey: Mmm,
now I see why you argued.
One rice cake is much heavier
than the other.
Oh! This will never do.
This will never do.
(*He takes a bite from the larger
rice cake.*) Now! That should
make them equal.

Narrator: He placed the rice cakes
on the scales again.
But the monkey had taken
such a big bite
that now the smaller rice cake
was too heavy.

Mr. Monkey: Oh, this will never do!

Narrator: Then Mr. Monkey took
a bite from the smaller rice cake.
But again he had taken
such a big bite that
once more, the larger rice cake
was too heavy.

Mr. Monkey: Oh dear. Oh dear.
This will never do!
*(He takes another bite from
the larger rice cake.)*

Tiger Cat (*looking worried*):
Ahem, Mr. Monkey, I'm sure
they must be equal by now.

Narrator: But again, Mr. Monkey had taken
such a big bite from the larger rice cake
that the smaller rice cake was now too heavy.

Tabby Cat: Please, please, don't trouble
yourself further, Mr. Monkey.
We really shouldn't have bothered you
with such a trifle.

Mr. Monkey: Oh no. It is no bother at all.
(*He takes another bite from
the smaller rice cake.*)

Narrator: Mr. Monkey went on,
weighing and biting
and weighing and biting,
until he had eaten both rice cakes
all up.
Then he looked at the two cats.

Mr. Monkey: Well, well. *(He licks his lips.)*
I said I could help you
and I hope that I have.
Now you have nothing at all
to argue about.

Narrator: And with a quick flick of his tail,
Mr. Monkey went off into the woods.

Tiger Cat *(looking extremely unhappy)*:
Oh, that cunning Mr. Monkey!
He's eaten both our rice cakes.

Tabby Cat *(also extremely unhappy)*:
And hasn't left even a crumb.

Tiger Cat: Not a crumb!

Tiger Cat and Tabby Cat:
EOOWRR. EOOWRR.
We've been tricked.
How foolish we are!
How foolish we are!

Tiger Cat and Tabby Cat:
  We're two foolish, silly, hungry cats.

Narrator: And they went off down the road
empty handed and hungry.
From that day,
they never argued again.

24